cross stitch

Tea Time
Sweet Models to Stitch

kanaviçe

Beş Çayı

Lesley Teare

Project Gallery
Proje Galerisi

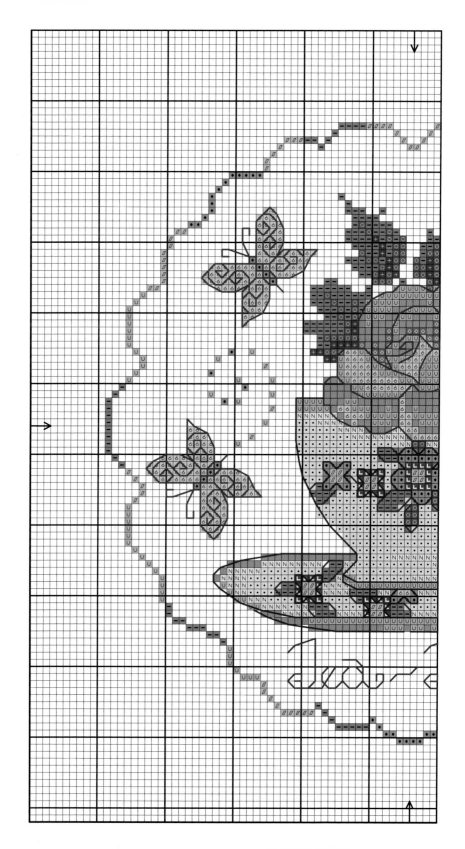

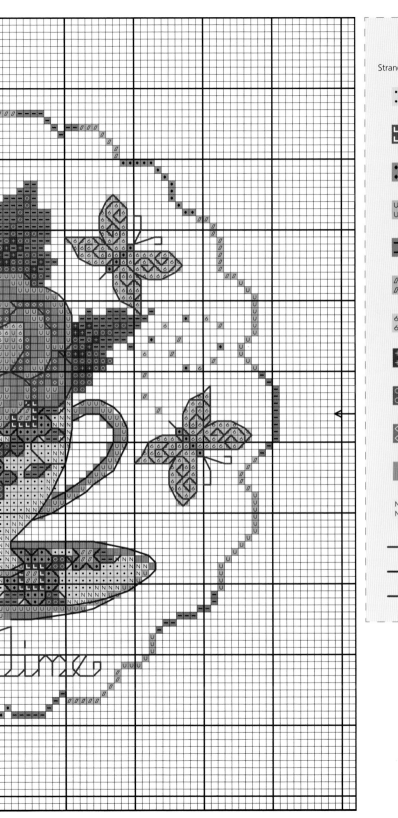

Mouliné
Stranded Cotton Art. 117

::		Ecru
ᴸᴸ		208
•:•		210
U U		605
▬		704
0 0		772
6 6		818
+ +		987
O O		988
◇ ◇		3705
▣		3706
N N N		3823
——		150
——		801
——		904

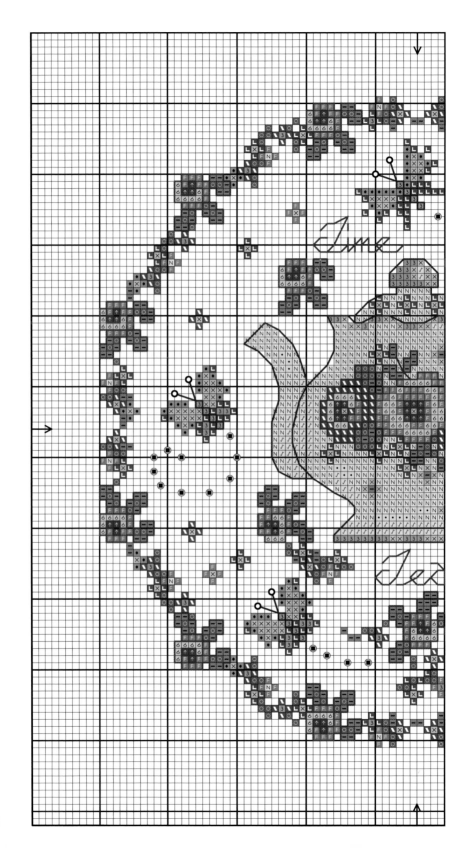

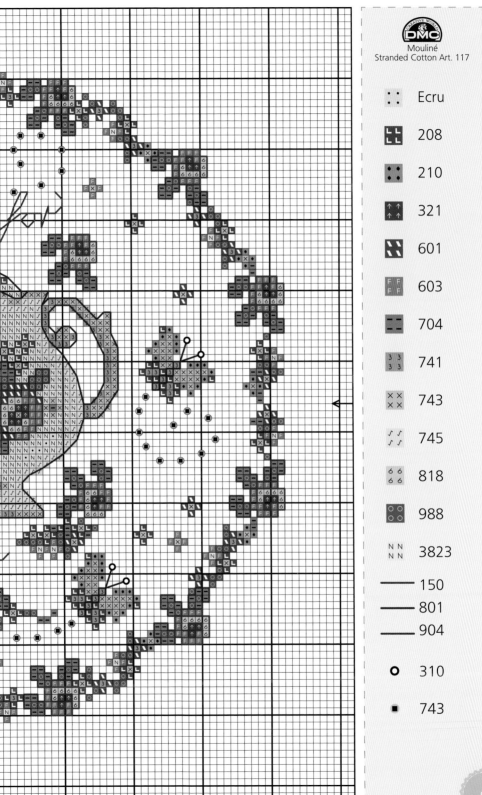

DMC
Mouliné
Stranded Cotton Art. 117

: :	Ecru
L L / L L	208
: :	210
↑ ↑ / ↑ ↑	321
N N	601
F F / F F	603
= =	704
3 3 / 3 3	741
X X / X X	743
∫ ∫ / ∫ ∫	745
6 6 / 6 6	818
O O / O O	988
N N / N N	3823
———	150
———	801
———	904
O	310
■	743

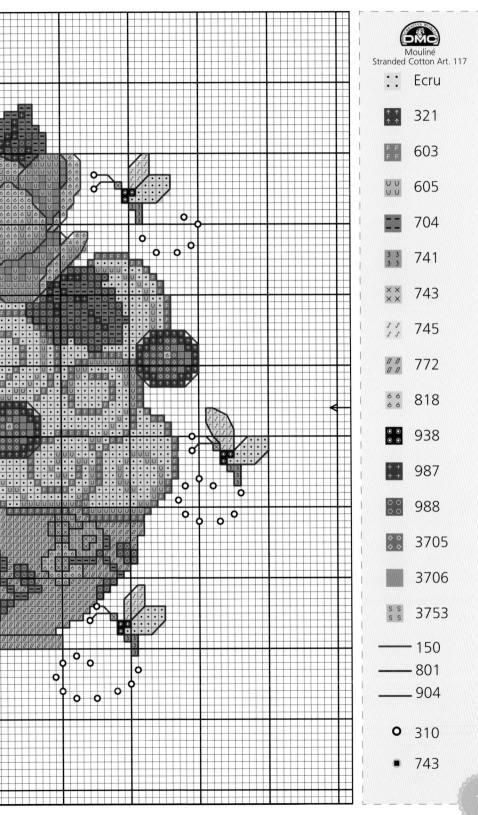

DMC
Mouliné
Stranded Cotton Art. 117

::	Ecru
↑↑ ↑↑	321
FF FF	603
UU UU	605
▬▬	704
33 33	741
×× ××	743
∕∕ ∕∕	745
⁄⁄ ⁄⁄	772
66 66	818
⦿⦿ ⦿⦿	938
++ ++	987
∘∘ ∘∘	988
◇◇ ◇◇	3705
■	3706
SS SS	3753
——	150
——	801
——	904
O	310
■	743

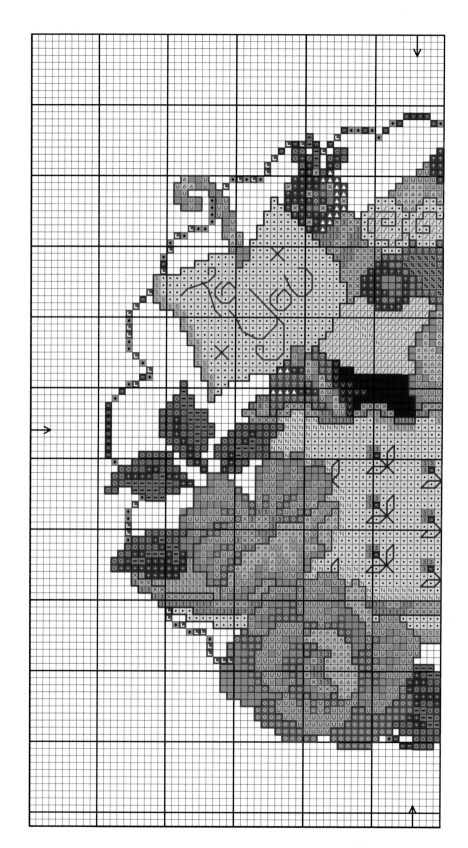

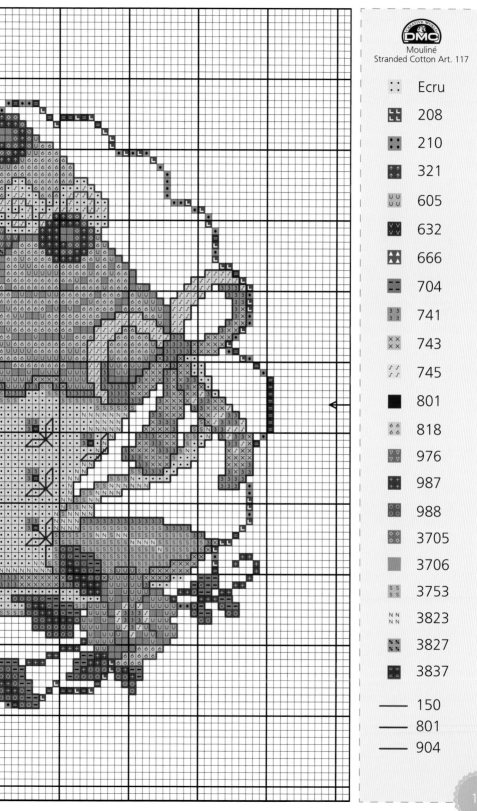

DMC Mouliné
Stranded Cotton Art. 117

::	Ecru
LL	208
••	210
↑↑	321
UU	605
VV	632
⋈⋈	666
▬▬	704
33	741
XX	743
⁄⁄	745
■	801
66	818
▽▽	976
++	987
○○	988
◇◇	3705
▦	3706
SS	3753
NN	3823
⁒⁒	3827
▤▤	3837
——	150
——	801
——	904

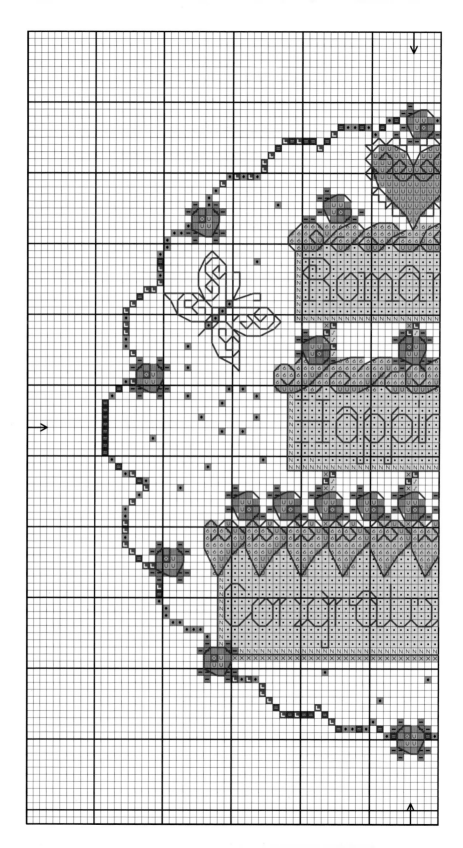

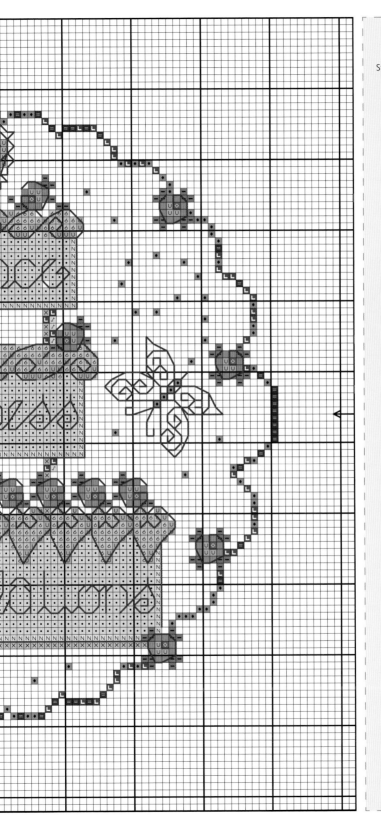

Mouliné
Stranded Cotton Art. 117

::	Ecru
LL	208
::	210
U U U	605
--	704
X X X X	743
∫ ∫ ∫ ∫	745
6 6 6 6	818
◇ ◇	3705
■	3706
N N N N	3823
■■ ■■	3837
——	150

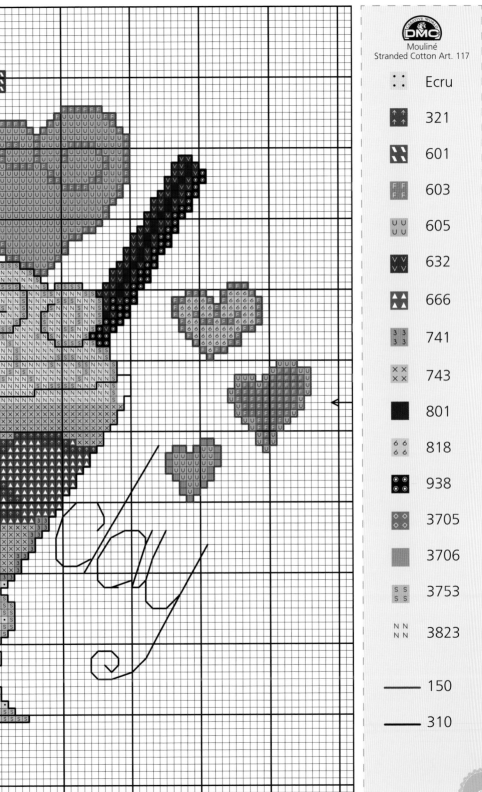

DMC
Mouliné
Stranded Cotton Art. 117

: :	Ecru
↑ ↑	321
❚❚	601
F F F	603
U U U	605
V V V	632
▲▲	666
3 3 3	741
× × × ×	743
■	801
6 6 6 6	818
● ● ● ●	938
◇ ◇ ◇	3705
▨	3706
S S S S	3753
N N N N	3823
——	150
——	310

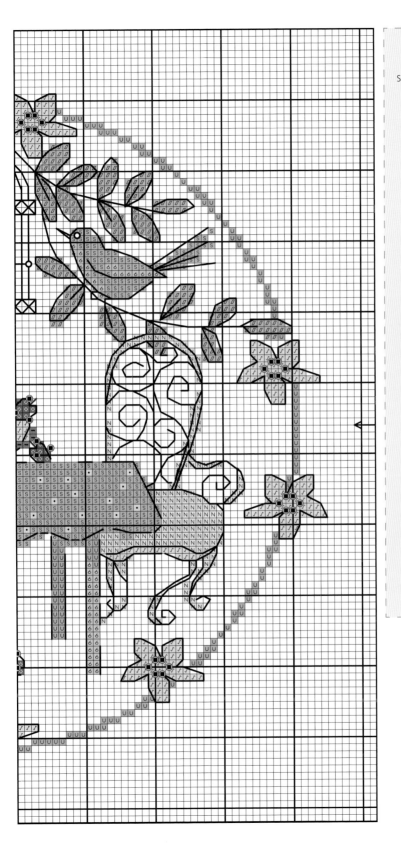

Mouliné
Stranded Cotton Art. 117

: :	Ecru
U U U U	605
▬ ▬	704
∫ ∫ ∫ ∫	745
⊘ ⊘ ⊘ ⊘	772
6 6 6 6	818
O O O O	988
◇ ◇ ◇ ◇	3705
S S S S	3753
N N N N	3823
——	310
——	904
O	310
■	743

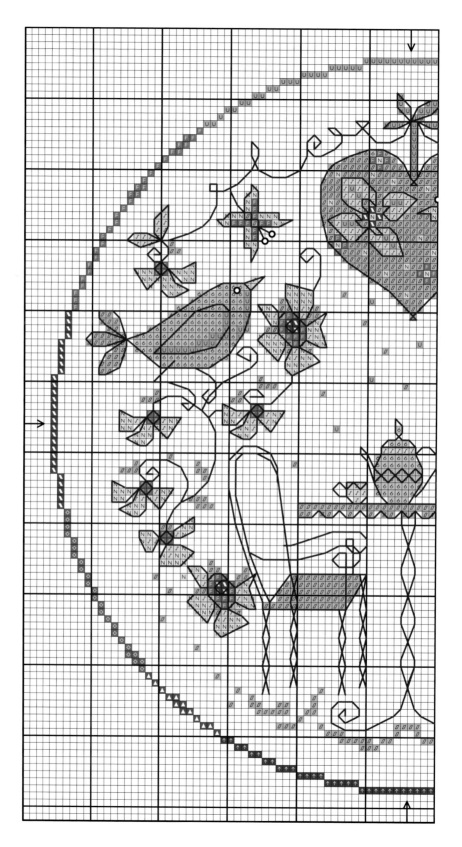

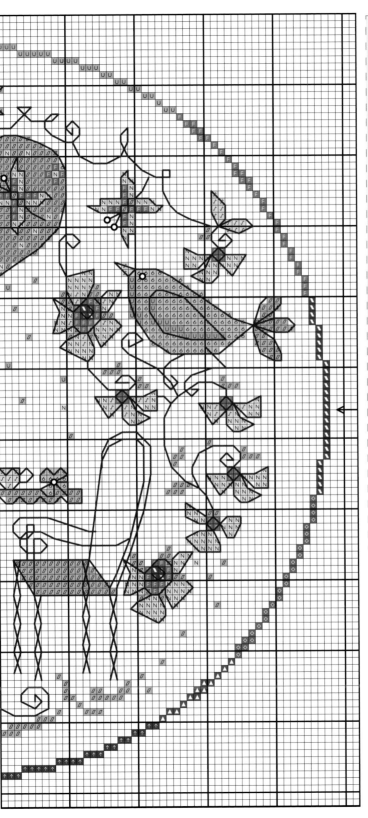

DMC
Mouliné
Stranded Cotton Art. 117

↑↑ ↑↑	321
◥◣ ◥◣	601
F F F F	603
U U U U	605
▲▲ ▲▲	666
∫ ∫ ∫ ∫	745
0 0 0 0	772
6 6 6 6	818
◇◇ ◇◇	3705
N N N N	3823
——	801
O	310

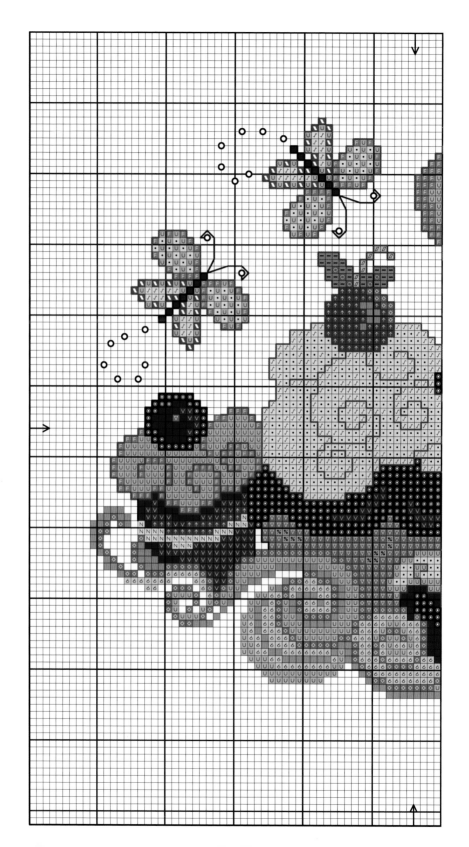

DMC
Mouliné
Stranded Cotton Art. 117

Symbol	Color
::	Ecru
↑↑	321
\\	601
F F	603
U U	605
V V	632
▬▬	704
∫∫	745
◊◊	772
■	801
6 6	818
●●	938
▽▽	976
○○	988
◊◊	3705
■	3706
N N	3823
✕✕	3827
——	150
——	310
——	904
○	310

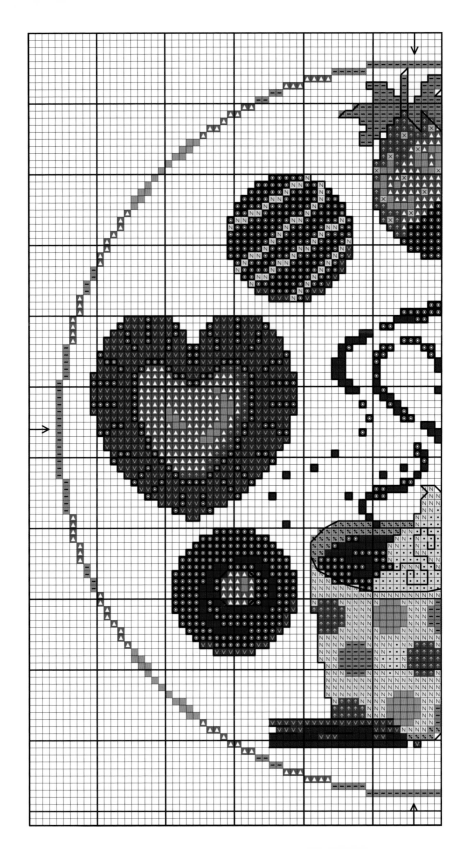

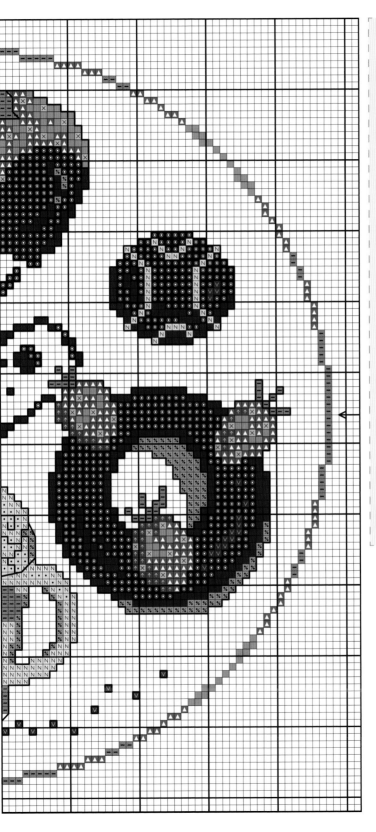

DMC
CREATIVE WORLD
Mouliné
Stranded Cotton Art. 117

	Ecru
↑ ↑ ↑ ↑	321
V V V V	632
▲ ▲	666
— —	704
× × × ×	743
■	801
⊙ ⊙ ⊙ ⊙	938
	3706
N N N N	3823
% % % %	3827
——	310

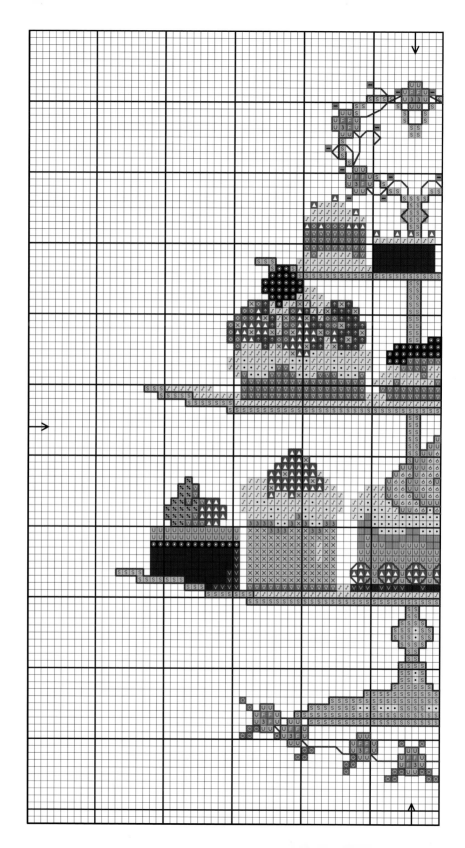

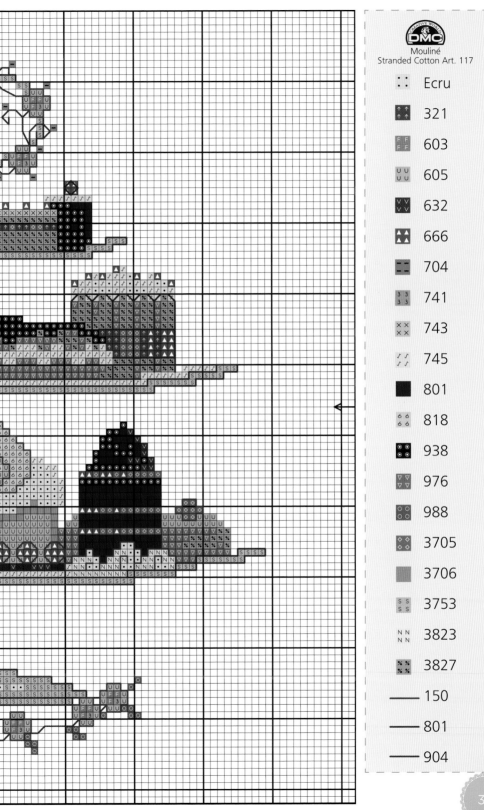

DMC
Mouliné
Stranded Cotton Art. 117

::	Ecru
↑↑	321
F F	603
U U	605
V V	632
▲▲	666
--	704
3 3	741
× ×	743
♪ ♪	745
■	801
6 6	818
● ●	938
▽ ▽	976
○ ○	988
◇ ◇	3705
■	3706
S S	3753
N N	3823
% %	3827
——	150
——	801
——	904

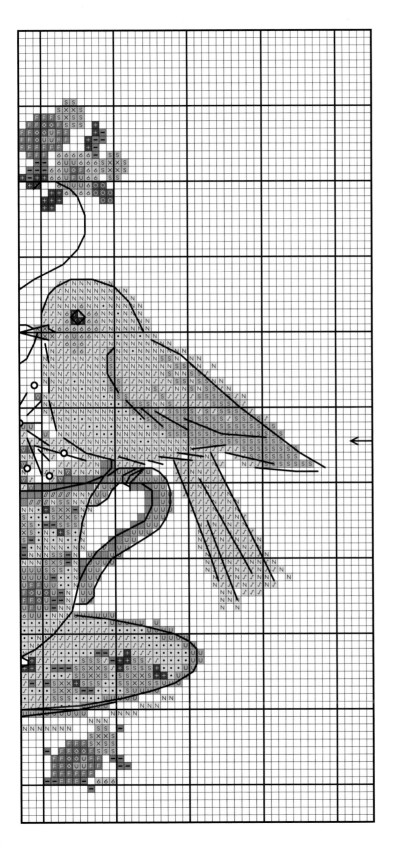

DMC
Mouliné
Stranded Cotton Art. 117

∵∵	Ecru
F F / F F	603
U U / U U	605
V V / V V	632
▬ ▬	704
× × / × ×	743
∫ ∫ / ∫ ∫	745
◫ ◫ / ◫ ◫	772
6 6 / 6 6	818
▽ ▽ / ▽ ▽	976
+ + / + +	987
○ ○ / ○ ○	988
◇ ◇ / ◇ ◇	3705
▦	3706
S S / S S	3753
N N / N N	3823
⁒ ⁒ / ⁒ ⁒	3827
▬▬▬	310
○	310

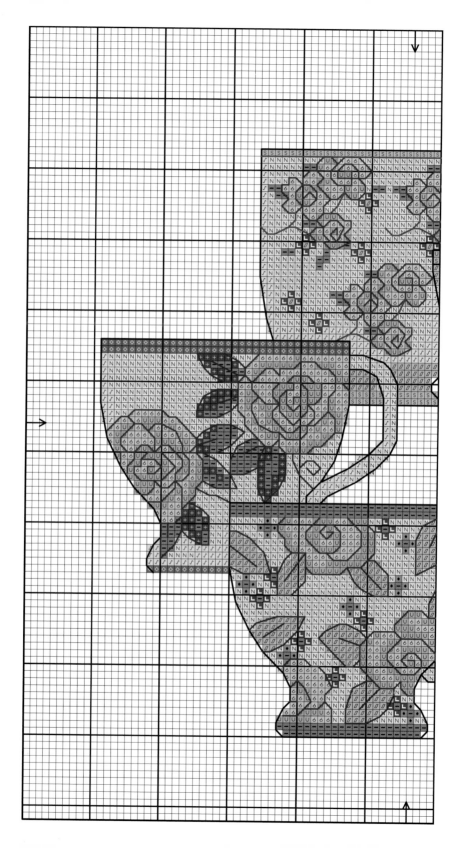

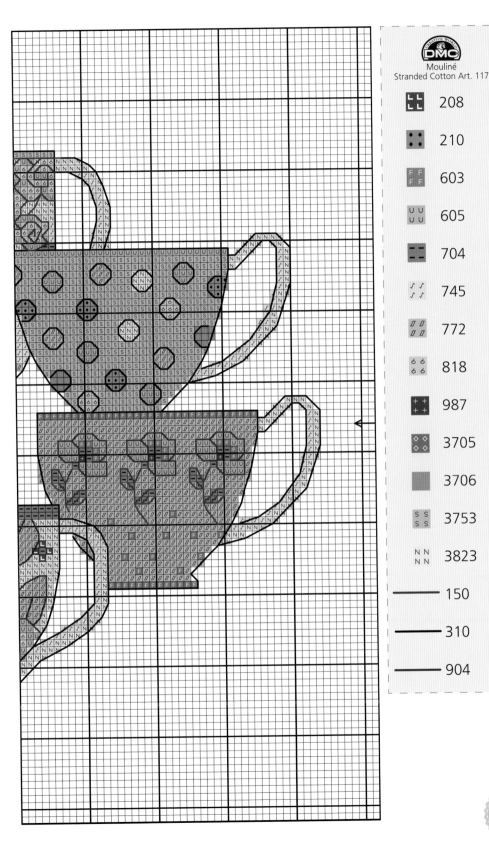

DMC
Mouliné
Stranded Cotton Art. 117

Symbol	Color
L L / L L	208
: :	210
F F / F F	603
U U / U U	605
– –	704
∫ ∫	745
0 0 / 0 0	772
6 6 / 6 6	818
+ + / + +	987
◊ ◊ / ◊ ◊	3705
■	3706
S S / S S	3753
N N / N N	3823
——	150
——	310
——	904

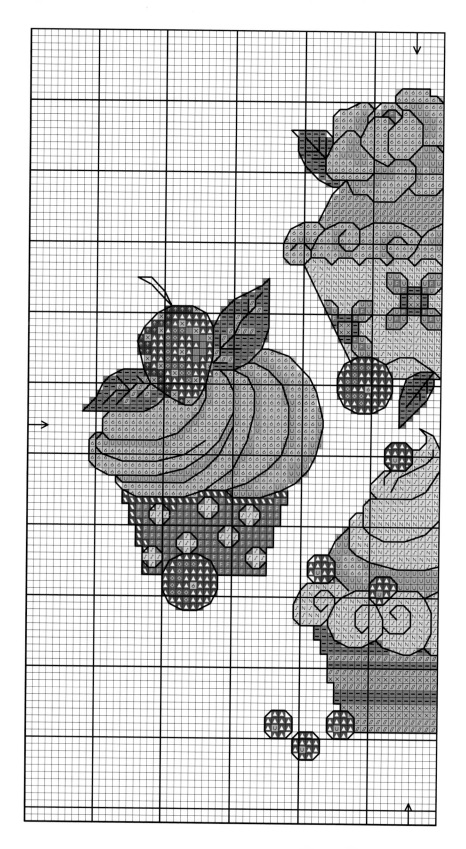

Mouliné
Stranded Cotton Art. 117

::	Ecru
LL	208
::	210
↑↑	321
✦✦	601
FF	603
UU	605
▲▲	666
▬▬	704
××	743
∕∕	745
⦸⦸	772
66	818
OO	988
◇◇	3705
■	3706
NN	3823
—	310

Please accept
my beautiful
congratulations

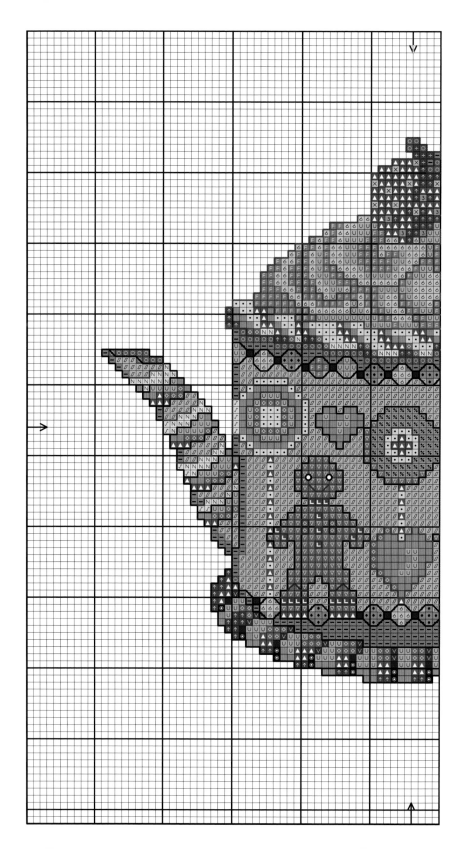

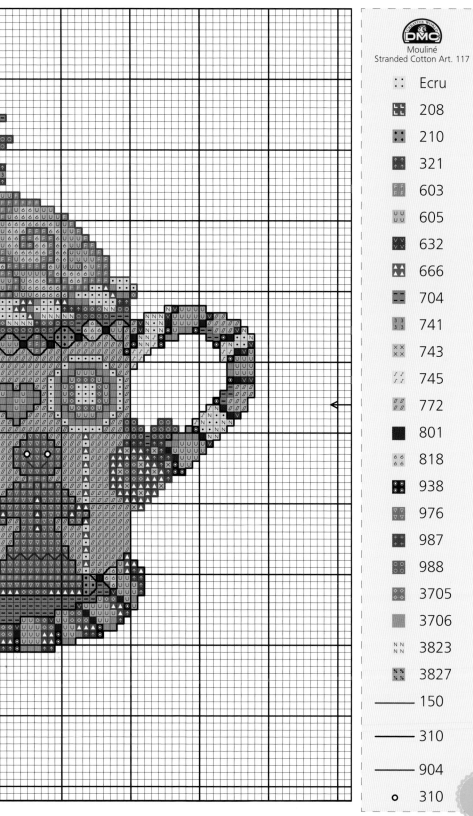

DMC
Mouliné
Stranded Cotton Art. 117

::	Ecru
	208
::	210
↑↑	321
F F	603
U U	605
V V	632
▲▲	666
--	704
3 3	741
X X	743
/ /	745
// //	772
■	801
6 6	818
••	938
▽▽	976
+ +	987
○ ○	988
◇ ◇	3705
	3706
N N	3823
◌ ◌	3827
——	150
——	310
——	904
○	310

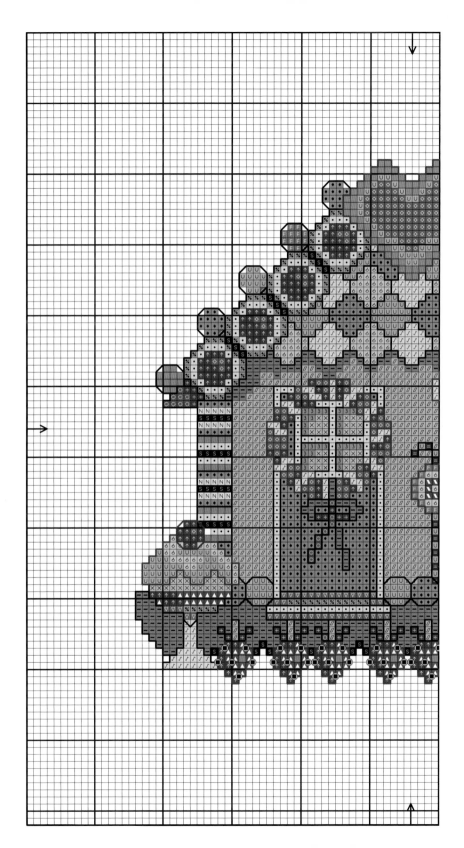

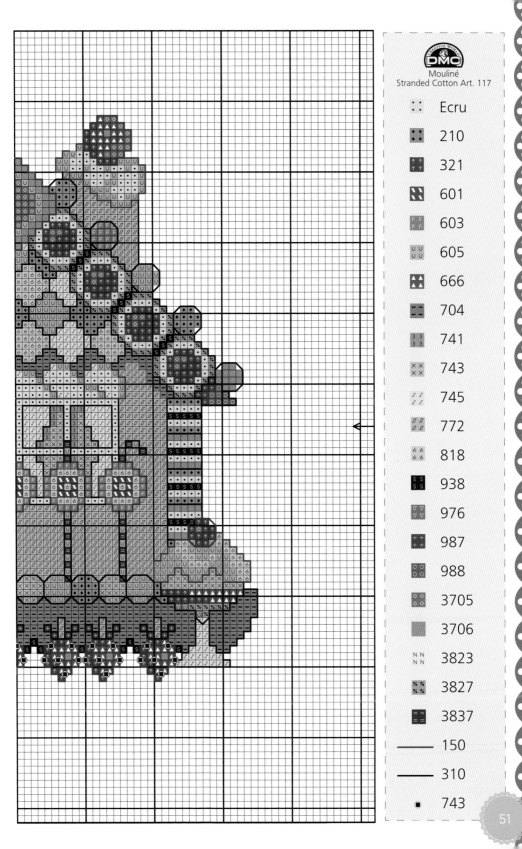

DMC
Mouliné
Stranded Cotton Art. 117

Symbol	Color
::	Ecru
••	210
↑↑	321
⟍⟍	601
F F	603
U U	605
▲▲	666
▬▬	704
3 3	741
× ×	743
⁄ ⁄	745
⫽ ⫽	772
6 6	818
S S	938
▽ ▽	976
+ +	987
○ ○	988
◇ ◇	3705
▪	3706
N N	3823
▓▓	3827
▬▬	3837
——	150
——	310
▪	743

Best Wishes

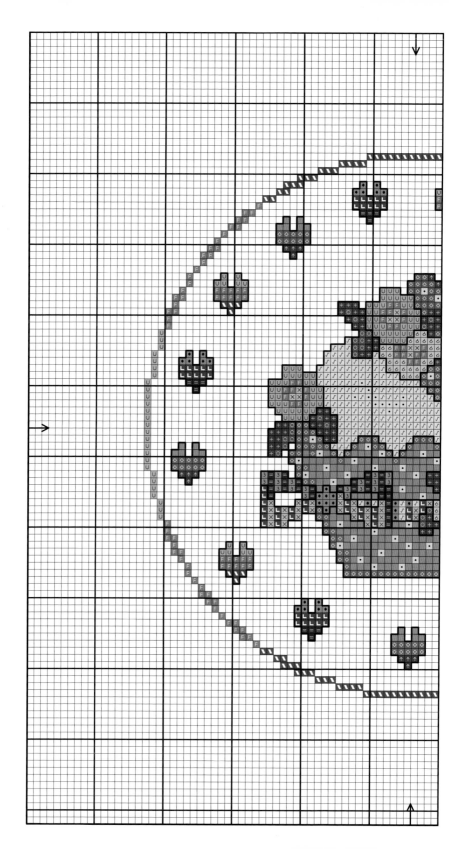

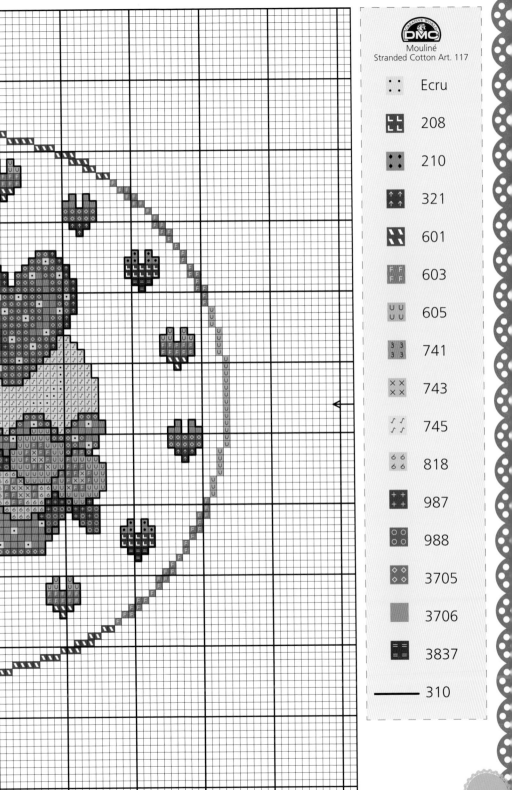

DMC
Mouliné
Stranded Cotton Art. 117

::	Ecru
LL LL	208
::	210
↑↑	321
◤◤	601
FF FF	603
UU UU	605
3 3 3 3	741
×× ××	743
∫∫	745
66 66	818
++ ++	987
OO OO	988
◇◇	3705
■	3706
≡≡	3837
▬▬	310

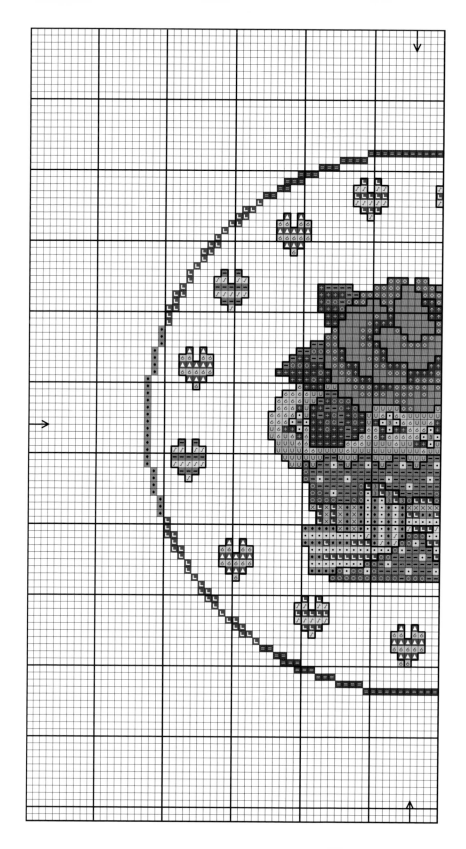

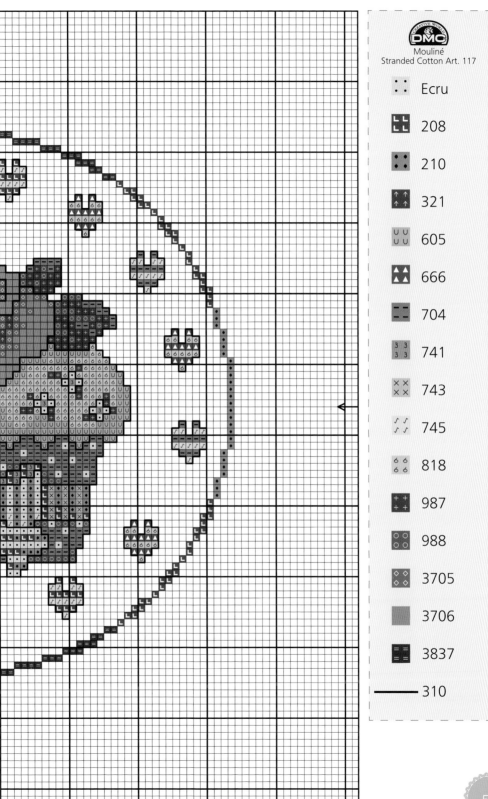

DMC
Mouliné
Stranded Cotton Art. 117

Symbol	Code
::	Ecru
LL LL	208
::	210
↑↑ ↑↑	321
U U U U	605
▲▲	666
══	704
3 3 3 3	741
×× ××	743
∕∕ ∕∕	745
6 6 6 6	818
++ ++	987
○○ ○○	988
◇◇ ◇◇	3705
▨	3706
══	3837
——	310

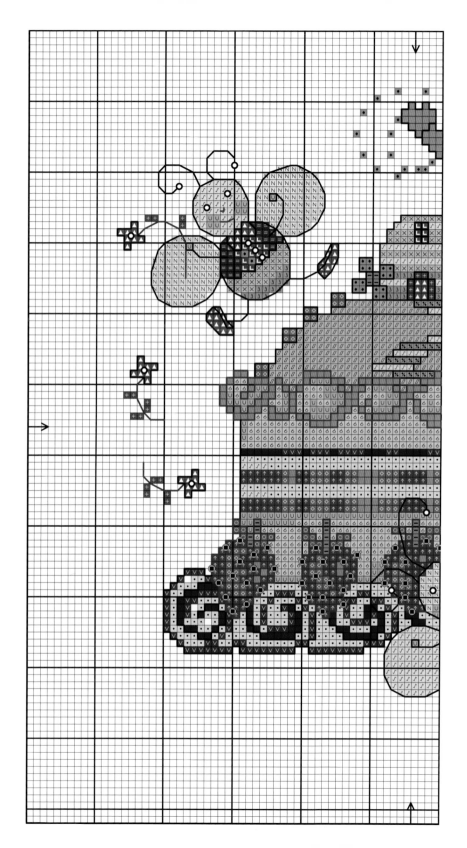

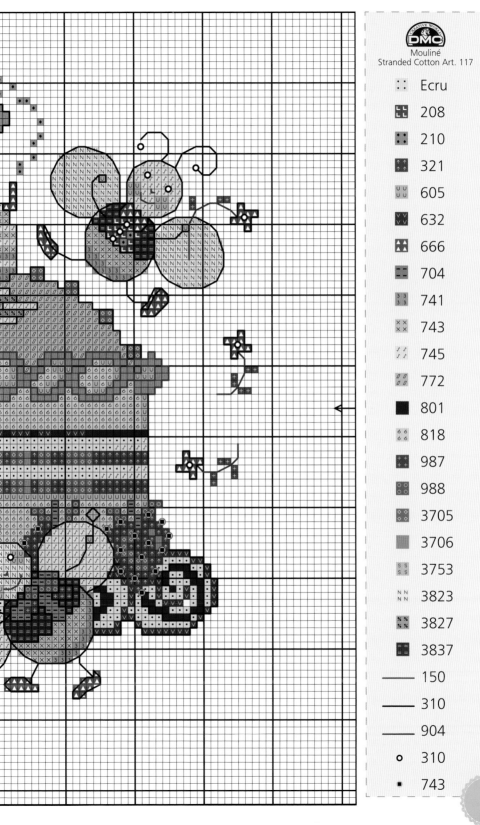

Mouliné
Stranded Cotton Art. 117

::	Ecru
🔲	208
⠒⠒	210
↑↑	321
U U	605
V V	632
▲▲	666
⚏	704
3 3	741
× ×	743
∕ ∕	745
∅ ∅	772
■	801
6 6	818
+ +	987
○ ○	988
◇ ◇	3705
▥	3706
S S	3753
N N	3823
⚌	3827
⚏	3837
——	150
——	310
——	904
○	310
•	743

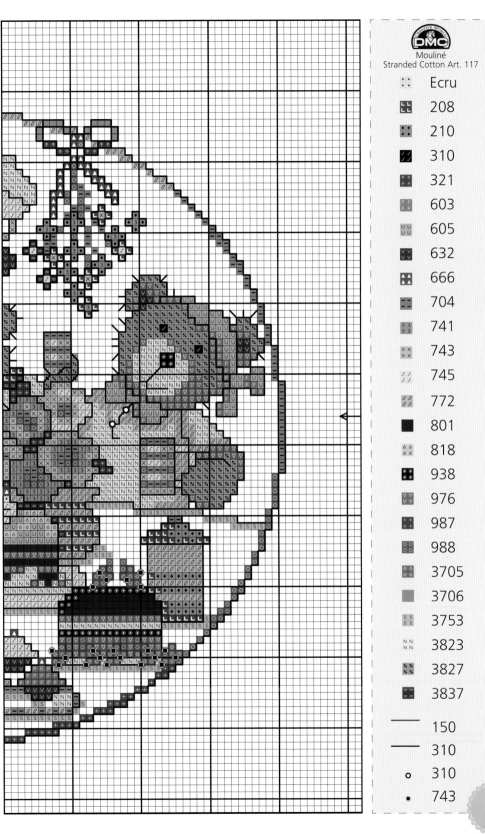

DMC
Mouliné
Stranded Cotton Art. 117

Symbol	Color
::	Ecru
ԼԼ	208
::	210
⟋⟋	310
↑↑	321
FF	603
UU	605
VV	632
▲▲	666
▬▬	704
3 3	741
✕✕	743
⟋⟋	745
⫽⫽	772
■	801
6 6	818
●●	938
▽▽	976
++	987
○○	988
◇◇	3705
▦	3706
S S	3753
N N	3823
✕✕	3827
▬▬	3837
——	150
——	310
○	310
▪	743